CONTENTS

Introduction 4

Why do people move? 6

A good move 12

Why moving can be hard 18

Repossession and eviction 24

Homelessness 30

Coping with moving 34

Moving on 40

Top ten tips for coping with moving 42

Glossary 44

Find out more 46

Index 48

⚠️ **Stay safe on the internet!**
When you are on the internet, never give personal details such as your real name, phone number, or address to anyone you have only had contact with online. If you are contacted by anyone who makes you feel uncomfortable or upset, don't reply to them, tell an adult, and block that person from contacting you again.

Any words appearing in the text in bold, **like this**, are explained in the glossary.

Introduction

Have you ever moved house? Maybe you have friends who have moved away or perhaps your own family is planning to move in the future. Members of your family might have moved away, leaving you behind. Would you like to move to a new place or does the idea fill you with worries? There can be many reasons why people move to a new area. Each move is a new beginning with its own opportunities and problems.

How this book can help

As you read this book you will find plenty of information about moving your belongings and starting out in a new place. There is also information to explain why some people are forced to move and how they deal with these situations. You will find practical tips to help you cope with moving away to a new home. For some people, moving can be an exciting adventure but for others it can be a sad, scary, or unsettling time.

BEHIND THE HEADLINES

One family that had to cope with moving to a new city was the Obama family. The US President's daughters, Malia and Sasha, had to say goodbye to their friends in Chicago and deal with a new life and school in Washington, D.C. Living in the White House might be luxurious and exciting, but their way of life has changed in other ways too. They can no longer just go out on their bikes to explore the neighbourhood. Moving can be hard for anyone, whatever their situation.

Moving house can involve a lot of hard work for all the family, but it can be exciting too.

Why do people move?

There are many reasons why people move. Some people choose to move to a new home. They might be moving away from home for the first time and leaving their family to go to university or to start a job. You may have an older brother or sister who has moved away from the family home. This can be difficult if you miss them but great if you get to move into their room!

Some families need to move into a bigger property so that they have more space for a growing family. Other families are forced to move to a smaller property or a home in a different area if they need to save money. Sometimes people have to move when parents separate or **divorce**, and families may need a larger home if they are going to live with a **step-parents** who have their own children. Some people move house to be closer to relatives who need help and care.

CASE STUDY

Many children find it is difficult to move when their parents split up. They might spend half their time in one home and half in the other, or might only visit one parent sometimes. When Ethan was 12 years old, he was unhappy that he had to move because his parents were getting divorced. In one summer, he had to move to a completely new area and get used to everything being new, including living with just his mum.

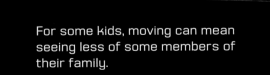

For some kids, moving can mean seeing less of some members of their family.

Moving for work

Another reason why many people have to move is because of a change at work. Many families have to move to a new area because a parent has a new job or their job has moved to a new place. Children with parents in the **military** will often have to move from one **military base** to another, sometimes even moving to a new country. They will only stay in a new place for a few years before they face another move.

Some people find they have to move to a new part of their country or a new country altogether because they can't find work where they live. This situation can sometimes mean a parent has to move away and leave the family behind.

It is okay to feel sad about moving far away from your old home.

These Chinese workers may have travelled from the countryside to work on building projects in the towns.

BEHIND THE HEADLINES

In China many people have moved to new places to work. As China's **economy** grew and many factories started making goods in the cities, millions of people moved from the countryside to find work. However, in 2009 there was a global **recession**. Money problems affected the whole world. This led to a lot of the factory work in China stopping. People who had worked in factory jobs had to move back to the countryside. Seventeen-year-old Quan Xiaoju had travelled thousands of miles to the city of Guangzhou to work in a factory that made jewellery to be sold abroad. When customers in other countries stopped buying the jewellery, Quan Xiaoju lost her job. She has had to move back to her village where she can live with family, but where there is no work. When the economy recovers she will move back to a city and start again.

Forced to move

Some people are forced to move for **economic** reasons. When people can no longer afford to pay for their home, they have to move out and find a new place to live. You can read more about this situation on pages 24 and 25.

Some people move because a situation that is out of their control forces them to go. In some countries people have to move away to a new place because of a war that threatens their safety. In other places natural disasters, such as hurricanes, floods, earthquakes, or volcanoes, destroy people's homes and force them to find a new place to live. Many of these people have to live in temporary camps to begin with. Sometimes they have to live in these camps for a long period of time.

BEHIND THE HEADLINES

On 12 January 2010 a huge earthquake hit Haiti, in the Caribbean. Hundreds of thousands of people died and many more were injured. At least 250,000 homes were destroyed or damaged beyond repair. This left more than a million people with nowhere to live. Many people were too poor to do anything other than set up makeshift camps in the capital city, Port-au-Prince, where they struggled for food and safety. Other people moved to smaller towns or villages to stay with relatives. They may end up staying in the villages and working on farms, because the factories where they used to work were destroyed in the earthquake. Some Haitians felt they would have to move to another country, such as the neighbouring Dominican Republic or the United States.

The earthquake in Haiti made many people homeless. They had to gather any of their belongings they could find amongst the rubble.

A good move

There are many positive things about moving to a new place. A fresh start can be exciting and you might discover new things about yourself that you would never learn if you stayed in one place.

Get sorted

Moving to a new place makes people sort through their belongings and decide what they still need. Before you start packing your things for a move, go through them and decide what can be given away or recycled. You might want to give some things to your friends to remind them of you. Other items could go to a charity shop or a car boot sale. Getting rid of some of your old stuff will make packing much easier and will help you prepare for a new start.

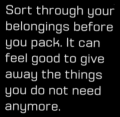

Sort through your belongings before you pack. It can feel good to give away the things you do not need anymore.

Selling things you no longer need is also a great way to make some money.

BEHIND THE HEADLINES

Recently, many people have been thinking about how we all need to cut down on the amount of stuff we own. The United States has only 5 per cent of the world's **population** but uses up 30 per cent of the world's **resources**. The United States also produces 30 per cent of the world's waste. This level of **consumption** can't go on, as the planet just doesn't have enough resources. People in the United Kingdom also need to get used to owning and using up less stuff. Remember this — for every dustbin full of rubbish you leave out for collection, there are around 70 dustbins full of the waste produced when the stuff in your bin was first made.

Get involved

Starting in a new school and neighbourhood gives you the chance to make new friends and try new activities. You have new places to explore, both in your local neighbourhood and in the wider area. Moving to a new country can mean a different culture and language. These changes can feel scary at first, but once you settle in, getting to know a new culture can be very rewarding. Learning a new language could be useful for many reasons, from making friends to building your future **career**.

Get out

If you feel lonely in a new place, go out and explore your new surroundings. Visit the tourist office and find out what is going on. Get to know the streets, shops, and other **facilities** in your area and you'll soon start to feel at home. It's a good idea to get information on clubs and activities that interest you, but you might want to settle in a bit before you sign up to do too many things.

Exploring your new area by bike is a good way to get to know the neighbourhood quickly.

Online!

The internet can help you to explore your new area. Go online at home or in your local library to find maps, directions, and information about the area. If you use **message boards** online to talk to local people, remember to be careful about giving out personal details. Never agree to meet anyone that you haven't ever met face to face.

Going online with a parent will help you find information that is most useful to you.

A new start

Throughout life you will find yourself in different situations where you have to get to know new people. These situations might include **exchange visits** or joining a new club. When people are older they may go to university or start a new job. Moving to a new place and making new friends can be difficult, but getting to know people is a skill you will always need.

Sometimes you will be glad to make new friends but if you already have good friends, you don't have to lose touch with them. You can call or write to your old friends, even while you're busy meeting new people in your new home. Making new friends will make you more confident and you will feel happier and braver next time you're in a new situation.

Don't worry if you feel left out at first. You will soon get to know people and make friends.

Sports and other activities are a great way to meet new people.

CASE STUDY

Anya has moved house several times. Her parents work in the **military**, so she has been to three different secondary schools. She finds it difficult to cope with so much change. She says it can seem as if things will never get better, but there are ways to cope. She visits old friends and they visit her in her new home, and that has helped her keep close friendships. She has also joined a volleyball team, and found that the practice helped her to forget about school and unwind.

Why moving can be hard

Once the excitement of a new place has worn off, it can be difficult settling into a new life. If you can find ways to cope with your new situation, you will be able to use these **strategies** many times in the future.

Packing and unpacking all your things when moving house can sometimes feel overwhelming.

Stressed adults

One difficult part of moving can be seeing your parents so stressed. They have many things to worry about, such as the **financial** cost of moving, the amount of organization, the tiring job of packing and moving all the family's possessions. They are probably also worrying about how the move will affect you. When your parents are feeling stressed these feelings can affect the whole family.

WHAT DO YOU THINK?

Is it better to get involved in the move yourself or should you just leave it to your parents?

Help out with it?	Keep out of it?
If you talk to your parents about the move, you'll all understand how everyone is feeling.	If you're unhappy about the move it might be better to keep quiet and avoid arguments.
If you help your family with the planning and packing, everyone will feel closer and less stressed.	If your parents are stressed it's best to keep out of their way.
If you join in with organizing the move you'll be more prepared when you get to your new home.	If you just focus on sorting out your own things you might feel you have more control.

Upside down

Many people find moving house stressful and upsetting. It can feel like your life is tipped upside down and you might have no idea where half your belongings are during the packing and unpacking. Sometimes things get lost during a move or it takes months before a box of things you need is found and unpacked.

It can be frustrating when all your things are packed up and you can't find what you need.

A new space

It can take a long time to feel settled in a new home and you might not have as much space or privacy as you did before. If you move to a smaller house, you might share a room with a sibling for the first time. If you move to live with a **step-parent**, you could have step-siblings to share your space with. It can take time to get used to these new arrangements. You might have lost a garden or other special place. You might feel you have nowhere private to go when you feel angry or sad.

Online!

There are online tools you can use to plan your space in a new home. You might be in a smaller bedroom so it will be more difficult to fit your furniture in. If you will be sharing a room, you might want to think about ways to create your own special space. Look at the websites on page 47 to get some ideas on how to organize your things in the space you have.

The internet can help make moving house easier and more fun.

Saying goodbye

Leaving people behind is a difficult part of moving house. Saying goodbye to friends, neighbours, teachers, and family can feel sad, especially if they are people you see most days. If you are settled and happy at school then you might wonder how you will fit in at a new school. Getting to know a new place and meeting people is not easy and you can feel lonely to start with. However difficult it feels, try to remember that things will get better. What you are going through will give you skills that will help you to cope in new situations all through your life.

Try to see saying goodbye as part of a new start.

You might be sad that you won't see some people every day but you can still visit and keep in touch.

CASE STUDY

When you move to a new place you can feel you are alone with your problems. In fact, everyone goes through similar feelings when they move away from people and places they know. Nathan moved from England to Australia and he was really scared at first. He didn't want to leave his grandma, friends, or school. However, Nathan loves his new house and after a while he made a lot of friends at his new school. He still misses his grandma but she is going to visit him. It was difficult to move at first but now he is settled and happy.

Over the last few years the whole world has been hit by a **financial** crisis that many people call the "**credit** crunch". The problems were partly started by banks and other organizations lending money to people to buy homes that they could not afford. Many people found they could not keep up with the payments on their **mortgages**. Suddenly it was difficult for people all over the world to borrow money. House prices then started to fall. This meant many people found their home was not worth as much money as they had paid for it. All of these problems and others led to a global **recession** that made it difficult for millions of people to keep their homes.

This bar chart shows that as the credit crunch hit, many more people were unable to keep up their mortgage payments, and so their homes were **repossessed**.

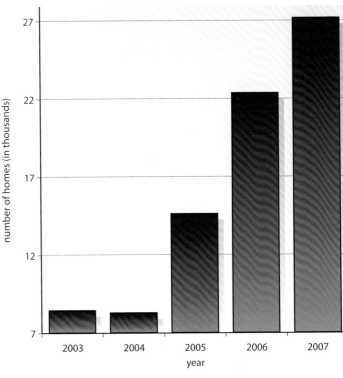

Number of homes repossessed in the United Kingdom because mortgages could not be paid, 2003–2007

number of homes (in thousands)

year

BEHIND THE HEADLINES

Towards the end of 2007, the news was full of stories about the credit crunch. Many stories were about **sub-prime mortgages**. These were mortgages where money had been lent to people to buy a home when they really had no hope of paying back the **loan**. When many people could no longer pay back their loans there was major panic. Many banks suddenly refused to give other customers any credit. Credit is needed to keep the **economy** and businesses working. When banks stopped lending money there were major problems that led to many people losing their jobs and homes.

The crisis meant that many mortgage lenders needed help from the government, while others closed down completely. Here, people are queuing to take their money out of their bank, as they fear it is about to close down.

How do mortgages work?

When people **rent** a property, they pay money every month to their landlord. The landlord owns their home and looks after it. When people buy a house, they usually need a loan called a mortgage. This is money that a bank or other financial organization lends them. The home buyer has to pay back the loan plus **interest** over a certain number of years. When people borrow money to buy a home they try to make sure they can afford the monthly payments so they can manage the mortgage. If everything goes to plan, the home buyer eventually pays back the loan in full and then their home belongs to them.

WHAT DO YOU THINK?

Do you think it is better to rent or buy?

Buying a home	Renting a home
You can decide how to decorate your home and what to do with it.	When you buy a home you have to pay for all the repairs. When you rent a home, your landlord has to do this.
Buying a home is an **investment**. When you have paid off the mortgage you will own it.	A mortgage is risky if your situation changes. When you rent, your monthly payments can be more predictable.
As you pay off more of the mortgage you will have less to pay each month.	It's easy to move on when you need to. Selling a house can be stressful and take up a lot of time.

Often people pay an estate agent to help them buy and sell a home. Estate agents put up "for sale" signs to advertise when a property is being sold.

What is repossession?

Unfortunately, sometimes things don't go to plan. The credit crunch made life difficult for millions of people. Many people lost their jobs. When they were unable to earn money, people could no longer pay their monthly mortgage payments and so they lost their homes. When the money lender takes someone's home because they can't repay the mortgage it is called repossession.

What is eviction?

Things can also go wrong for people who rent a home. People who lose their jobs can often no longer pay their rent. If their landlord has financial problems and can't afford their own mortgage, the people living in the rented house may have to move out. When someone who rents is forced to move out of his or her home it is called **eviction**.

It can be devastating to find out you must move out of your home.

People who are forced to move out of their home face the pressure of finding somewhere new to live.

CASE STUDY

The Gray family was hit hard by the credit crunch. Both parents are **self-employed**, which means they work for themselves instead of working as part of a bigger company. Robert Gray plays and teaches the guitar and Rachel Gray teaches drama and looks after their two children. When problems with the economy started, many of their pupils suddenly couldn't afford lessons. The Grays couldn't pay their mortgage. The family of four had to move out when their house was repossessed. They couldn't find a home to rent because they were self-employed and landlords thought they wouldn't be able to pay the rent. Luckily, the Grays could move in with grandparents until they sorted themselves out. Otherwise they would have had nowhere to live.

Homelessness

Do you think homeless people live only on the streets of big cities? In fact, many other people are also homeless. Some are staying with friends or family, or living in a bed and breakfast or shelter. People can become homeless when they have money problems or lose their jobs. They might struggle to find new work or a cheaper home and end up with nowhere to live. Families can become homeless when parents split up. Often they are only homeless for a while, but it can be very scary.

Natural disasters can leave many people around the world homeless. Earthquakes, floods, and hurricanes are events that people have no control over. These disasters destroy huge areas, leaving governments with the hard and costly task of rebuilding.

BEHIND THE HEADLINES

Hurricane Katrina hit the city of New Orleans, USA in August 2005. The hurricane left 80 per cent of the city flooded for weeks and many people were left homeless. Thousands of homes were destroyed at a cost of around £59 billion. To start with, many homeless people were put in cruise ships, hotels, and **military bases**. This housing was expensive and unpopular so families were moved into temporary trailers and apartments while the city was rebuilt. However, the **credit** crunch made things worse by slowing down the building of new homes in New Orleans. By 2009, nearly 20,000 families were still living in temporary **accommodation**, waiting for a permanent home to move into.

Hurricane Katrina destroyed thousands of homes. Here, a girl and her grandmother are gathering their belongings from amongst the wreckage of their home.

A helping hand

In poor countries, families who are made homeless by war or disasters can have nowhere to live for a very long time. But in **developed** countries, such as the United Kingdom, most families only face homelessness for a short time. Many people start by moving in with relatives or friends, or have access to a special shelter.

There are organizations that help people who lose their homes. The charity Shelter supports and advises anyone in this situation. Families can also talk to their local council about new housing and often they will be put on a waiting list. While they are waiting, families should be given help with paying for somewhere safe and secure to live. Homelessness can be very upsetting for young people, who may move far away from their school and friends.

Luckily, most people have family and friends to stay with if they find themselves without a home.

CASE STUDY

Amie's dad worked abroad and was doing well until his business failed. The family had to move back to London, but they had nowhere to live. They ended up in a hostel shared with 100 other people. Amie thinks she is lucky not to be living on the streets, but the hostel can feel very cramped and she can't listen to loud music or be herself. Her brother misses having lots of toys and clothes because they don't have much money left after paying for rent and transport. Amie is just one of around 130,000 young people in the United Kingdom who don't have a home of their own.

All families want somewhere safe and secure for their children to live.

Coping with moving

If your family is moving, you probably have a mixture of feelings. You could be excited about going somewhere new and meeting different people. But you might also feel sad and anxious about the changes you are facing.

Let your parents know how you feel about moving.

Keep talking

Whatever you are feeling, remember that you can cope with moving. Make sure you understand the reasons why your family is moving. You might feel angry or upset, but there might be very good reasons why you have to move. Talk to your parents about how you feel and any worries you have. It is important that everyone understands and supports each other to help make the move less stressful for everyone.

WHAT DO YOU THINK?

If you are angry about moving, talking to your parents might be the last thing you feel like doing. But if you are upset, talking to someone might help you to cope.

If you talk about how you feel...	If you don't talk about how you feel...
... the things you are worrying about might not seem so serious.	... the things you are worrying about might seem like bigger problems than they really are.
... you'll find other people feel the same as you and this can make you feel better.	... you can feel very lonely and anxious.
... you might find ways to deal with the problems together.	... you'll stay focused on the problems and it might be hard to move on.

Getting organized

If you accept that you are moving and organize yourself and your belongings, you will feel in control and happier. Sort your things into different piles: things you are going to need close by during the move, things that you will want to unpack soon, and things that you can pack away and deal with later. Keep a checklist of what is included in each box and number the boxes. Then you can ask for certain boxes to be put in a place you can easily get to and quickly find anything you need.

Unpacking

When you unpack, don't open all the boxes and tip everything on the floor. Work through one box at a time and find a place for everything before you start on the next box. Unpacking this way will help you feel in control and you'll start to feel at home in your new room.

CASE STUDY

When James moved to a new town, he packed the bag he was going to keep with him all the time. As well as clean clothes, pyjamas, and a toothbrush, he put a book, his games console, photos of his friends, and some snacks in this bag. "Moving house is really boring. My mum and dad were busy for ages so it was good to have stuff to do and things to eat if I got hungry." James also made sure his skateboard and bike were unpacked quickly so that he could go outside and explore his new street.

Getting organized before the move will make you feel much calmer.

Keep in touch

Many people who move feel sad about leaving friends behind. If you are moving far away, then you might wonder when you will see your friends again. Remember, you don't have to say goodbye forever. You could have a leaving book that your friends can sign and write messages in. A class photo will help you to remember your school friends, or you could take photos of people and places at your old school. Get an address book and write down the addresses, phone numbers, and email addresses of anyone you want to keep in touch with. Don't wait until the day before you move to do this!

New friends

Even if you miss your old friends, try not to let these feelings stop you from making new friends. A good way to meet people is to join clubs, activities, and sports teams. If everyone at your new school already knows each other it might take a while to make friends, but don't give up. Remind yourself it will take time and give people a chance to get to know you.

Online!

The internet is a great way to keep in touch with the friends you have left behind. Catching up on social networking sites is the quickest and easiest way to stay in regular contact with each other. You can upload photos to show your friends what your new home is like. Avoid chat rooms where people you don't know might try to contact you.

Having a chat on the phone with an old friend can be relaxing after trying to get to know new people.

Moving on

Everyone can find moving difficult. If you feel angry, sad, or confused about moving house, then you are not unusual or alone. The best way of coping is to keep talking to your family and friends about how you feel. Try not to focus on what you have left behind. Instead, look for ways to keep yourself busy. If you get out and spend time with other people, you will feel much better than if you stay indoors by yourself.

WHAT DO YOU THINK?
Would it be better if you never had to move house?

Better to move?	Better to never move?
You discover new places and perhaps learn about new cultures and languages.	Everything is familiar and you can easily find your way around.
You make new friends and can still keep in touch with the old ones.	You grow up with the same group of friends.
Getting to know new places and people can make you more confident.	You feel safe and don't have to talk to people you don't know.
You sort out your stuff and recycle things you don't need any more.	You can keep everything from your childhood.

All through your life, there will be changes and you will find ways to deal with them. Leaving friends behind doesn't mean that you have lost those friends. When you make new friends, you aren't replacing old friends. You'll just have more friends than before. And that can't be a bad thing, can it?

Once your family has settled in, your old friends might be able to visit you in your new house.

Top ten tips for coping with moving

Whatever the reasons are for moving house, you will probably find the change difficult at times. Here are some tips to help you cope as you settle into your new life:

1.   Make sure you are clear about why your family is moving house. If you don't understand why you are moving, the changes involved in moving can be more difficult to accept.

2.   Find out as much as you can about the place you are moving to. Look at your new school's website and visit the school if you can. Research your new area and think about the things you would like to do there.

3.   If you feel very upset about moving, tell someone how you are feeling. If you can't tell a parent, then talk to a teacher or a counsellor at an organization such as ChildLine (details on page 47).

4.   Be as organized as you can. If you plan your packing and know where things you need are, you will feel much more in control.

5.   Make sure you have the contact details of people you want to keep in touch with before you leave. You might want to take an address book to school during the weeks before you leave so you have plenty of time to do this.

6.   Make a list of things you are excited about before you move. When you feel sad or lonely, look at the list you made and remind yourself what you were looking forward to about your new home.

7.   Find a club or activity you can join in your new neighbourhood. Don't give up if you don't make new friends straight away – remember that it can take time.

8. If you have questions about your new school, you could write to or email your new teacher before you move. Always ask them if you are unsure about anything once you start at the new school.

9. If you are feeling lonely, don't stay at home on your own. Go out for a walk or a bike ride and explore a new place.

10. Keep in touch with your old friends. If they come to visit you, show them all around your new area so they know as much as possible about your new life.

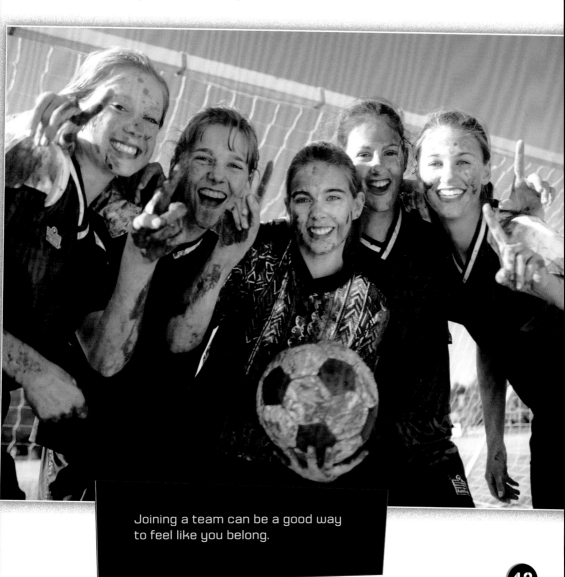

Joining a team can be a good way to feel like you belong.

Glossary

accommodation place to live

career type of work someone chooses to do

consumption buying and using things up

credit money that is lent to people or businesses

developed country that has a stable economy, industry, and a relatively comfortable standard of living

divorce ending of a marriage by a court of law

economic relating to the economy

economy system that manages money, and the production and trade of goods

eviction removal of people from a rented home

exchange visit stay with the family of a friend in another country, followed by a visit in return

facilities places and services that people use in their day-to-day lives

financial to do with money

interest payment made for the use of money or credit, usually a percentage of the amount used

investment use of money to gain more in return

loan anything that is lent by one person or organization to another, for example money

message board website that allows people to share useful information

military to do with the army, air force, or navy

military base place where members of the military live and train

mortgage loan of money to buy a house

population number of people living in a place

recession situation where there is less business being done and less money being earned than previously

rent payment made to a landlord so people can live in a home

repossession when a mortgage lender takes a house or flat from a borrower

resources materials and energy provided by the Earth and Sun

self-employed someone who earns money through their own business

step-parent person who marries a child's mother or father

strategy plan or way of dealing with a situation

sub-prime mortgage loan to buy a house made to a borrower who is likely to have trouble paying the money back

Find out more

Books

The Bed and Breakfast Star, Jacqueline Wilson (Yearling, 2006)

Homelessness (Talk About), Kaye Stearman (Wayland, 2008)

Moving (Separations), Janine Amos (Cherrytree Books, 2008)

The Moving Book: A Kid's Survival Guide, Gabriel Davis
(First Books, 2008)

Moving House (Tough Topics), Patricia Murphy
(Heinemann Library, 2008)

Websites and organizations

The following websites and organizations can help you get settled in your new home and offer support to help you cope with moving:

earth.google.co.uk
Visit this website to download Google Earth and take a look at your new home and area from the air!

**kids.discovery.com/fansites/tradingspaceskids/roommaker/
roommaker.html**
This fun website will give you ideas about decorating your new room.

**roomplanner.icovia.com/bedsbunksandlofts/resources/
icovia.aspx**
This website might be useful to help you plan the space in a new home or bedroom.

shelter.org.uk
Visit the Shelter website to find out more about homelessness.

www.childline.org.uk
Telephone: 0800 1111
If you feel anxious or upset about moving, you might want to contact ChildLine and chat to someone. ChildLine has trained counsellors who give advice, support, and information on a range of issues. Calls are free and won't appear on the phone bill. Visit their website to find out how to email their counsellors or chat to them online. You can also write to ChildLine at Freepost 1111, London, N1 0BR (no stamp needed).

www.dec.org.uk
The Disasters Emergency Committee website has information about people affected by disasters around the world.

www.discovernorthernireland.com
If you are moving to somewhere in Northern Ireland, this website will give you information on interesting places to visit in your area.

www.itsnotyourfault.org
If you're moving house because your parents are splitting up you might find it useful to visit this website.

www.streetmap.co.uk
You can use this website to find a map of your new local area. Then you can go out and explore.

www.visitbritain.com/en/Things-to-do/
You can find out about interesting places to visit in your new neighbourhood on this website.

Index

address book 38, 42

chat rooms 38
ChildLine 42, 47
China 9
clubs and activities 14, 16, 17, 38, 42
confidence 16, 40
consumption 13
contact, keeping in 16, 17, 38, 42, 43
costs of moving 19
credit crunch 24–25, 28, 29, 30
cultures, new 14, 40

divorce 6

economic reasons for moving 8,
    9, 11
emails 38
eviction 28
exchange visits 16

facilities 14
forced moves 10–11
friends 16, 17, 23, 38, 40, 41, 43

goodbye, saying 22, 38

Haiti 11
homelessness 30–33
hostels 33
Hurricane Katrina 30

language learning 14, 40
leaving book 38
loneliness 14, 43

message boards 15
military families 8, 17
mortgages 24, 25, 26, 28, 29

natural disasters 10–11, 30, 32
neighbourhoods 14

Obama family 4
online information and advice 15,
    21, 46–47
organizing yourself 36, 42

packing 19, 20, 36, 42
parents 19
positive things about moving 12,
    14, 40, 42

reasons for moving 6–11, 42
recession 9, 24–25
recycling belongings 12, 40
rented homes 26, 28
repossession 24, 28, 29
researching a new area 42
rubbish 13

schools 14, 17, 22, 38, 42, 43
self-employment 29

smaller homes 6, 21
sorting belongings 12, 36
step-families 6, 21
stress 19, 20, 26
sub-prime mortgages 25

unpacking 20, 36

war 10, 32
work, moving for 8–9